Presented to

On the Occasion of

From

Date

© 2001 by Barbour Publishing, Inc.

ISBN 1-58660-118-0

All scripture quotations are taken from the King James Version of the Bible.

Published by Barbour Publishing, Inc., P.O. Box 719, Uhrichsville, Ohio 44683
http://www.barbourbooks.com

Member of the
Evangelical Christian
Publishers Association

Printed in Canada.

THE LITTLE BOOK OF
PRAYER

Compiled by
RICHARD A. HASLER

BARBOUR
PUBLISHING, INC.
Uhrichsville, Ohio

Contents

Adoration sets the tone for the entire prayer.
It reminds us Whom we are addressing,
Whose presence we have entered,
Whose attention we have gained.

BILL HYBELS
Too Busy Not to Pray

All great prayer, all liberating worship,
all lasting encounters with God,
begin with praise and rejoicing.

LLOYD OGILVIE
Let God Love You

Yank some of the groans out of your prayers,
and shove in some shouts.

BILLY SUNDAY

The sooner I forget myself in the desire
that He may be glorified,
the richer will the blessing be
that prayer will bring to myself.

ANDREW MURRAY
With Christ in the School of Prayer

God makes us covenant partners in the working out
of his purposes in the world,
and yet we are not equal partners.
God is the senior partner and
must therefore be approached
in awe and reverence.

DONALD G. BLOESCH
The Struggle of Prayer

Prayer is for the religious life
what original research is for science—
by it we get direct contact with reality.

P. T. FORSYTH
The Soul of Prayer

Are you so identified with the Lord's life
that you are simply a child of God,
continually talking to Him and
realizing all things come from His hands?

OSWALD CHAMBERS
My Utmost for His Highest

The spirit of prayer makes us
so intimate with God that we
scarcely pass through an experience
before we speak to Him about it.

O. HALLESBY
Prayer

If you are God's child,
there is this expectant line of communication
always between you and God.
Your experience may be a dreary wilderness,
a sea of despair, a dusty, sandy waste with no shade—
but over all is a line of communication
between you and God.

OSWALD CHAMBERS
The Place of Help

Mental prayer is nothing else. . .
but being on terms of friendship with God,
frequently conversing in secret with Him.

TERESA OF AVILA
Life of St. Teresa

But at last it is truer to say
that we live the Christian life in order to
pray than that we pray in order to
live the Christian life.

P. T. FORSYTH
The Soul of Prayer

No evil habit is so ingrained
nor so long prayed against (as it seemed) in vain,
that it cannot, even in dry old age,
be whisked away.

C. S. Lewis
Letters to Malcolm: Chiefly on Prayer

This daily prayer for forgiveness
represents the washing of the hands and feet
of the wayfarer which have been stained and soiled
by the mud and dust of the journey.

C. F. ANDREWS
Christ and Prayer

Prayer abases intellect and pride,
crucifies vainglory,
and signs our spiritual bankruptcy,
and all these are hard for flesh and blood to bear.

E. M. BOUNDS
Power through Prayer

Let me call attention to that prayer of David,
in which he says:
"Search me, O God, and know my heart. . . ."
If we should all honestly make this prayer
once every day there would be a good deal
of change in our lives.
"Search me"—not my neighbor.

D. L. MOODY
Prevailing Prayer

The worst sin is prayerlessness.

P. T. FORSYTH
The Soul of Prayer

If your prayers are not being answered,
search your heart,
and see if there is someone you have yet to forgive.

LEHMAN STRAUSS
Sense and Nonsense about Prayer

Is there not something un-Christian
in rising from confession still in grey weather,
and without the sunshine having broken through?

ARTHUR GOSSIP
In the Secret Place of the Most High

Prayer is literally
talking things over in confidence—
in full confidence with God.
Sometimes the substitution of
the word "confidence" for
the word "faith" helps.

EUGENIA PRICE
Leave Yourself Alone

Prayers are heard in heaven
very much in proportion to our faith.
Little faith will get very great mercies,
but great faith still greater.

CHARLES H. SPURGEON
Gleanings Among the Sheaves: Believing Prayer

It does not make sense
to pray without faith.

LEHMAN STRAUSS
Sense and Nonsense about Prayer

The man is perfect in faith who can
come to God in the utter dearth of
his feelings and desires,
without a glow or an inspiration,
with the weight of low thoughts, failures, neglects,
and wandering forgetfulness,
and say to Him, "Thou art my refuge."

GEORGE MACDONALD
Unspoken Sermons

Prayer is a focus upon God
whereby all things come into focus.
By centering attention upon God the center,
all things become centered.

Eugene Peterson
Reversed Thunder: The Revelation of John and the Praying Imagination

Prayer is an effort of the will,
and the great battle in prayer is
the overcoming of mental woolgathering.
We put things down to the devil when
we should put them down to our
inability to concentrate.

OSWALD CHAMBERS
The Place of Help

Our cooperation with God is our receptivity,
but it is an active, a laborious receptivity,
an importunity that drains our strength away.

P. T. FORSYTH
The Soul of Prayer

Oh, to pray with a distinct object!
Indefinite praying is a waste of breath.

CHARLES H. SPURGEON
Barbed Arrows

Let him never cease from prayer
who has once begun it,
be his life ever so wicked;
for prayer is the way to amend it,
and without prayer such amendment
will be much more difficult.

TERESA OF AVILA
Autobiography

Our Lord's first public act was prayer:
"As he prayed the heavens were opened."
The last act of the Crucified before
giving up His life in atonement
for the world's sin was prayer.

OSWALD J. HOFFMAN
Life Crucified

During the course of the day,
I frequently ask the Lord to give me wisdom
to use the knowledge that I have and
to give me perspective and understanding,
particularly when difficult situations arise.

BEN CARSON, M.D.
Think Big

I have often wished that
I was a more decent man. . . .
Nevertheless, amid the
greatest difficulties of my administration,
when I could not see any other resort,
I would place my whole reliance upon God.

ABRAHAM LINCOLN
Letter to Baltimore Presbyterian Synod

I can worry myself into a state of
spiritual ennui over questions like
"What good does it do to pray
if God already knows everything?"
Jesus silences such questions.
He prayed; so should we.

PHILIP YANCEY
The Jesus I Never Knew

All healing is looked upon by
the Bible as a victory of God. . . .
He accepts all our prayers
for the healing of the sick.

PAUL TOURNIER
The Adventure of Living

God cares about every area of our lives,
and God wants us to ask for help.

BEN CARSON, M.D.
Think Big

If God doesn't seem to be giving you what you ask,
maybe he's giving you something else.

FREDERICK BUECHNER
Wishful Thinking

Worry about nothing; pray about everything.

CHARLES SWINDOLL
Laugh Again

I ask you neither for health nor for sickness,
for life nor for death;
but you may dispose of my health and my sickness,
my life and my death, for your glory.

BLAISE PASCAL

I pray that our Heavenly Father may assuage
the anguish of your bereavement
and leave you only the cherished memory
of the loved and lost
and the solemn pride that must be yours,
to have laid so costly a sacrifice
upon the altar of Freedom.

ABRAHAM LINCOLN
Letter to Lydia Bixby on loss of her sons in battle

What do you think about death,
about the death of your loved ones
and of yourself?
Talk with the Lord;
He understands and loves you.
Are you afraid? Give your fears to Him.

CORRIE TEN BOON
He Cares, He Comforts

God whispers to us in our pleasures,
    speaks in our conscience,
    but shouts in our pains;
it is His megaphone to rouse a deaf world.

C. S. LEWIS
The Problem of Pain

Prayer is the coming into awareness,
the practicing of attention,
the nurturing and development of
personal intensity before God.

EUGENE PETERSON
Reversed Thunder: The Revelation of John and the Praying Imagination

I never preach a sermon until
I have soaked it in prayer.

BILLY SUNDAY

True prayer is not to be found in
the words of the mouth
but in the thoughts of the heart.

GREGORY THE GREAT
Commentary on the Book of Job

We always have God's full attention.
Our part is to give Him ours.

EUGENIA PRICE
Leave Yourself Alone

As the saying goes:
He who thinks of many things
thinks of nothing and accomplishes no good.
How much more must prayer possess the heart
exclusively and completely if it is to be a good prayer.

MARTIN LUTHER
A Simple Way to Pray, for a Good Friend

Too many of our prayers—
private and public—
are just browsing amongst possible petitions,
not down to cases at all.
We expect nothing from our prayers
except perhaps a euphoric feeling.

CATHERINE MARSHALL
Adventures in Prayer

Commonly, those who pray long in a meeting do so,
not because they have the spirit of prayer,
but because they have not.
They should keep to the point
and pray for what they came to pray for
and not follow the imagination of
their own hearts all over the universe.

CHARLES FINNEY
Lectures on Revivals of Religion

If we are not entirely dedicated
to our own prayers,
we should not expect God
to waste time with us.

CHARLES L. ALLEN
Prayer Changes Things

Intercession means that we rouse ourselves up
to get the mind of Christ about the one
for whom we pray.

OSWALD CHAMBERS
My Utmost for His Highest

[The] prayer of intercession connects
God and other people:
it is one of the purest forms of service,
the mightiest single power on earth.
When we pray for others,
we open the pipeline to both ends,
and God flows through to bless
those for whom we pray.

FRANK LAUBACH
Channels of Spiritual Power

There is nothing that makes us love a man
so much as praying for him. . . .
By considering yourself as an advocate with
God for your neighbors and acquaintances,
you would never find it hard to be
at peace with them yourself.

WILLIAM LAW
A Serious Call

The Lord could do without our
intercession and our praise.
Yet it is the mystery of God that he should require us,
his coworkers, to keep on praying
and never lose heart.

ROGER SCHUTZ
The Rule of Taizé

Our hands are so tiny
and the world's needs so vast
that we are forced back upon God,
who alone is sufficient.

ARTHUR GOSSIP
In the Secret Place of the Most High

When was the last time you wrote somebody
and mentioned what you were
praying for on their behalf?

CHARLES SWINDOLL
Laugh Again

What is the value of praying for
the poor if all the rest of our time and interest
is given only to becoming rich?

P. T. FORSYTH
The Soul of Prayer

Pray to Him for me as I pray to Him for you.
I hope to see Him quickly.

BROTHER LAWRENCE
The Practice of the Presence of God

. . .trusting in Him, Who can go with me
and remain with you and be everywhere for good;
let us confidently hope that all will yet be well.
To His care commending you,
as I hope in your prayers you will commend me,
I bid you an affectionate farewell.

ABRAHAM LINCOLN
*Parting Address to friends in Springfield, Illinois,
February 11, 1861*

But Thou, taking Thy own secret counsel
and noting the real point to [my mother's] desire,
didst not grant what she was then asking
in order to grant to her the thing
she had always been asking.

St. Augustine
Confessions

A Christian fellowship lives and exists
by the intercession of its members
for one another, or it collapses.
I can no longer condemn
or hate a brother for whom I pray,
no matter how much trouble he causes me.

DIETRICH BONHOEFFER
Life Together

Real prayer is
life creating and life changing.

RICHARD FOSTER
The Disciplines of Prayer

Prayer that does not bear fruit in
self-giving service is not Christian prayer
but only soliloquy.

DONALD G. BLOESCH
The Struggle of Prayer

God grant that I may
never live to be useless!

JOHN WESLEY
Journal, June 28, 1783

The quality of a man's prayer is
determined by the state of his living.

WATCHMAN NEE
The Spiritual Man

Pray so that there is a real continuity
between your prayer and
your whole actual life.

P. T. FORSYTH
The Soul of Prayer

It is not so true that
"prayer changes things"
as that prayer changes me,
and I change things.

OSWALD CHAMBERS
My Utmost for His Highest

Prayer is not a method of using God;
rather is prayer a means of
reporting for duty to God.

CHARLES L. ALLEN
Prayer Changes Things

Meditation is not optional.
The same Bible that commands us to
"pray without ceasing," to "rejoice everymore,"
and "in everything give thanks". . .
also urges us to meditate.

CHARLES SWINDOLL
Growing Strong in the Seasons of Life

Seek God, not happiness—
this is the fundamental rule of all meditation.

DIETRICH BONHOEFFER
Life Together

The margins of one Bible after another
have literally been covered by the notes
I have been accustomed to making
along the way in my quiet time.

E. STANLEY JONES
The Divine Yes

Rich prayer is kindled with biblical knowledge.
Knowing the rich promises of God
in Scripture always provides a relevant stand
on which one can plead before God.

HAROLD CARTER
The Prayer Tradition of Black People

I see that prayerlessness is one
of my greatest sins of omission.
I am too short, ask too little,
ask too much want of forethought. . .
too little meditation upon Scripture.

ANDREW BONAR
The Diary and Life of Andrew Bonar

Don't take too much upon yourself
lest the spirit should get tired. . . .
It is sufficient to grasp one part from which
you can strike a spark in your heart.

MARTIN LUTHER
A Simple Way to Pray, for a Good Friend

Any method, absolutely any method, is your method
if you find it opens the doors toward heaven
and helps you gain contact with God.
And it is not your method,
no matter who does it,
if it does not succeed in doing that.

FRANK LAUBACH
Channels of Spiritual Power

The carpet in front of the mirrors
of some of you people is worn threadbare,
while at the side of your bed where
you should kneel in prayer
it is as good as the day you put it down.

BILLY SUNDAY

Do you wish to pray in the temple?
Pray in your own heart.
But begin by being God's temple,
for He will listen to those who
invoke Him in His temple.

St. Augustine

Every time that is not seized upon
by some other duty is
seasonable enough for prayer.

JEREMY TAYLOR
Holy Living

Love to pray—
feel often during the day the need for prayer,
and take trouble to pray.
Prayer enlarges the heart until it is
capable of containing God's gift of Himself.

MOTHER TERESA
A Gift for God

I live in the spirit of prayer.
I pray as I walk,
when I lie down, and when I rise.
And the answers are always coming.

GEORGE MÜLLER
An Hour with George Müller

Common prayer does not
dispense us from private prayer.
The one sustains the other.
Let us each day take time to renew
our personal intimacy with Jesus Christ.

ROGER SCHUTZ
The Rule of Taizé

And we must recognize that we are
heard not for our much speaking
but for our purity of heart.
Therefore our prayer must be brief and pure—
unless it chance be prolonged with
the inspiration of God's grace.

BENEDICT OF NURSIA
Rule of Saint Benedict

. . .the Lord's Prayer.
What is shorter to hear or read?
What is more easily memorized?

ST. AUGUSTINE
Enchiridion

For to this day I drink of
the Lord's Prayer like a child—
drink and eat like an old man;
I can never get enough of it.
To me it is the best of all prayers,
even above the Psalms,
though I love them very much.

MARTIN LUTHER
A Simple Way to Pray, for a Good Friend

Model

"Thy will be done on earth as it is in heaven."
When you say this in your pew on Sunday,
it means nothing unless you live it on Monday.

BILLY SUNDAY

The Lord's Prayer, in the King James Version,
contains only sixty-six words.
It can be repeated in less than a minute.
Despite its brevity,
it has been an enormous benefit to multitudes
of men and women.

W. PHILIP KELLER
A Layman Looks at the Lord's Prayer

Truly, no other can ever be found
that equals this [the Lord's Prayer] in perfection,
much less surpasses it.

JOHN CALVIN
Institutes of the Christian Religion

Finally, mark this,
that you must always make the amen strong,
never doubting that God is surely listening to you
with all grace and saying "Yes" to your prayer.

MARTIN LUTHER
A Simple Way to Pray, for a Good Friend

It is only the sentimentalists who
depict prayer as a perpetual April.
A good deal of prayer is framed in fall and winter,
and much of the real work of prayer is
best done in those very seasons.

DOUGLAS STEERE
Dimensions of Prayer

. . .nothing is so costly, so exorbitant, so extortionate,
as that which is bought by prayer.
While, on the other hand,
nothing is so truly and everlastingly enriching
as that which is gotten and held by prayer,
and by prayer alone.

ALEXANDER WHYTE
Lord, Teach Us to Pray

. . .always His timing.
We force and try to hurry
the divine schedule at our peril.

CATHERINE MARSHALL
Adventures in Prayer

God's best gifts, like valuable jewels,
are kept under lock and key,
and those who want them must,
with fervent faith, importunately ask for them;
for God is a rewarder of them
that diligently seek Him.

D. L. MOODY
Moody's Stories, Volume 2

One of the most liberating experiences
of my life came when I understood that
prayer involved a learning process.
I was set free to question,
to experiment, even to fail,
for I knew I was learning.

RICHARD FOSTER
Celebration of Disciplines

Be importunate, Jesus says—
not, one assumes,
because you have to beat a path to
God's door before he'll open it,
but because until you beat the path
maybe there's no way to getting to your door.

FREDERICK BUECHNER
Wishful Thinking

True prayer uncovers the
emptiness in the petitioner
but the fullness in the Petitioned.

WATCHMAN NEE
The Spiritual Man

I'm not asking why our petitions are so often refused.
Anyone can see in general that this must be so.
In our ignorance we ask what is not good
for us or for others,
or not even intrinsically possible.

C. S. LEWIS
Letters to Malcolm: Chiefly on Prayer

Keep close to the New Testament Christ,
and then ask for anything
you desire in that contact.

P. T. FORSYTH
The Soul of Prayer

Lord, what can I do to help You today?

RUTH BELL GRAHAM
It's My Turn

Many people would be greatly surprised if
God did answer their prayers.

D. L. MOODY
Prevailing Prayer

A PRAYER TO BE SAID WHEN
THE WORLD HAS GOTTEN YOU DOWN
AND YOU FEEL ROTTEN,
AND YOU'RE TOO DOGGONE TIRED TO PRAY,
AND YOU'RE IN A BIG HURRY, AND BESIDES,
YOU'RE MAD AT EVERYBODY: HELP

CHARLES SWINDOLL
Growing Strong in the Seasons of Life

O praise God for all you have,
and trust Him for all you want!

JOHN WESLEY
Letter to Alexander Knox,
July 11, 1778

Many a man will make
promises to God in his extremity
but forget them in his prosperity.

BILLY SUNDAY

Let me know Thee, O my Knower;
let me know Thee even as I am known.
O Strength of my soul,
enter it, and prepare it for Thyself
that Thou mayest have and hold it,
without "spot or blemish."

ST. AUGUSTINE
Confessions

Prayer is to be studied—
If I had an invitation to visit the queen and was told
I might ask what I pleased of Her Majesty,
I should prepare my request. . . .
When you go before God,
it is well to know what you want.

CHARLES H. SPURGEON
Barbed Arrows

God is the thing to which he is praying—
the goal he is trying to reach.
God is also the thing inside him
which is pushing him on—
the motive power.

C. S. LEWIS
Mere Christianity

If only God will enable me
to tend the possible,
depending on Him for the impossible.

RUTH BELL GRAHAM
It's My Turn

When you get whacked with a problem,
open yourself to a deeper relationship to the Lord.
Don't focus on the problem
but on the Lord's presence and power.

LLOYD OGILVIE
Let God Love You

If you are a stranger to prayer,
you are a stranger to the greatest source
of power known to human beings.

BILLY SUNDAY

Someone has said that when we work, we work,
but when we pray, God works.

BILL HYBELS
Too Busy Not To Pray

No one can believe how powerful prayer is and what it is able to effect except those who have learned it by experience.

MARTIN LUTHER
Table Talk

Prayer is spiritual dynamite.

HELEN SMITH SHOEMAKER
The Secret of Effective Prayer

A prayerless Christian is
a powerless Christian.

BILLY GRAHAM
Peace with God

Most Christians for most of the Christian centuries
have learned to pray by praying the Psalms.

EUGENE PETERSON
The Message: Psalms

The psalmists, in telling everyone
to praise God, are doing what all men do
when they speak of what they care about.

C. S. LEWIS
Reflections on the Psalms

It is therefore easy to understand why
the Book of Psalms is the favorite book of all the saints.
For every man on every occasion
can find in it Psalms which fit his needs,
which he feels to be as appropriate as if
they had been set there just for his sake.

MARTIN LUTHER
Preface to the Psalms

One of the values in becoming familiar with
the Psalms is that they gradually
become our own prayers.
When we meditate on the Psalms
with some regularity, we find that they
express our own feelings.

WILLIAM O. PAULSELL
Taste and See

The Psalms are the school for people learning to pray.
Fundamentally, prayer is our response
to God Who speaks to us.
God's Word is always first.
He gets the first word in, always.
We answer.

EUGENE PETERSON
Under the Unpredictable Plant

Let us recollect for whom and for what
we prayed in secret this morning–
or did not pray.
Let us recall what we read,
what we heard, and with what feelings–
with Whom we conversed, and about what. . . .

ALEXANDER WHYTE
Lord, Teach Us to Pray

In my experience,
the practice of written meditation can be of great help
in bridging the gap between our two worlds,
the spiritual and the material. . . .
Writing something down also makes it more real.
If I do not write,
my meditation is likely to
remain vague and nebulous.

PAUL TOURNIER
The Adventure of Living

Self-centered prayers become manifestly self-centered,
even to us, when seen on paper.
Insights that are hazy figures on the horizon
sometimes become crystal clear when
committed to a journal.

RICHARD FOSTER
Freedom of Simplicity

If you are willing to commit your prayer to paper,
you probably really mean it. . . .
To write it down is one step in self-committal.

E. STANLEY JONES
Abundant Living

I suggest that we try listening to God
on the border lines of sleep. . . .
Many writers have a pen and paper ready
at their bedsides to record their inspirations
before their treacherous memories lose
what comes to them.

FRANK LAUBACH
Channels of Spiritual Power

The Lord let in much light.
Many sweet truths I wrote down.

THOMAS SHEPARD
Meditations

If the Holy Spirit should come when these thoughts are
in your mind and begin to preach to your heart,
giving you rich and enlightened thoughts,
then give Him his honor. Let your preconceived ideas go;
be quiet and listen to Him Who can talk better than you,
and note what He proclaims and write it down,
so will you experience miracles.

MARTIN LUTHER
A Simple Way to Pray, for a Good Friend

I proceeded further in reading my
old private writings and found that they had
the same effect upon me as before.
I could not but rejoice and bless God
for what passed long ago,
which, without writing, had been entirely lost.

DAVID BRAINERD
Memoirs

At the end of each month
I read over my prayer journal and see
where God had done miraculous things. . . .
If I can list a number of answers to
specific prayers in January,
I feel better prepared to trust God in February.

BILL HYBELS
Too Busy Not to Pray

To be "silent unto God" does not mean
drifting into mere feeling or sinking into reverse,
but deliberately getting into the center of things
and focusing on God.

OSWALD CHAMBERS
The Place of Help

The stilled voice learns to hold to peace;
to listen with the heart to silence, that is joy.

MADELEINE L'ENGLE
The Weather of the Heart

Inward silence renders
possible our conversation with Jesus Christ.

ROGER SCHUTZ
The Rule of Taizé

Get alone with God.
Seek some secluded spot.
Close the inner door to the inner room
of your inner spirit.
Be still. Be silent. Be serene.

W. PHILIP KELLER
Walking with God

Before there can be meaningful conversation with God,
we must take time to wait on the Lord
in silent expectation.

DONALD G. BLOESCH
The Struggle of Prayer

We need the channel of silence to transport us
from the busy harbors of our own tensions
out to the ocean of God's infinite being.

MARVA J. DAWN
Reaching Out without Dumbing Down

In silence and quiet, the devout soul profiteth
and learneth the secrets of the Scriptures.

THOMAS À KEMPIS
The Imitation of Christ

Two friends can be together in the silence
with genuine creativity in solace or joy or supplication.
In my heart, I ask Him to do this or that.
He also asks me.

EUGENIA PRICE
Another Day

God's methods don't change because
we are so noisy and busy.
He is longing for your attention,
your individual and full attention. . . .
He will wait and wait until
you finally sit in silence and listen.

CHARLES SWINDOLL,
Growing Strong in the Seasons of Life

We are silent at the beginning of the day
because God should have the first word,
and we are silent before going to sleep
because the last word also belongs to God.

DIETRICH BONHOEFFER
Life Together

Prayer is not a means by which
I seek to control God;
it is a means of putting myself in
a position where God can control me.

CHARLES L. ALLEN
Prayer Changes Things

I will renounce my will, my inclinations,
my whims and fancies
and make myself a willing slave
to the will of God.

MOTHER TERESA
A Gift for God

I would a thousand times rather that God's will
should be done than my own.
I cannot see into the future as God can;
therefore, it is a good deal better to let Him choose
for me than to choose for myself.

D. L. MOODY
Prevailing Prayer

The people of true prayer are those who
can see the answer when it is given in God's way,
not theirs.

HELEN SMITH SHOEMAKER
The Secret of Effective Prayer

I have often found that what I sought most
I did not get at the right time,
not till it was too late,
not till I had learned to do without it,
till I had renounced it in principle
(though not in desire).

P. T. FORSYTH
The Soul of Prayer

God will be responsible for our feelings
if we will hand them over to Him.

CATHERINE MARSHALL
Something More

Prayer, at long last, is an altar and an oblation. . . .
By this surrender prayer finds a
"service which is perfect freedom."
In this loss, prayer wins its richest gain.

GEORGE A. BUTTRICK
Prayer

Had a most fervent wrestle with the Lord tonight. . . .
I wanted to wear out my life in His service,
and for His glory.

DAVID BRAINERD
Memoirs

When we omit thanksgiving from our prayers,
we rob God of an honor due Him,
and we render our prayers powerless.

LEHMAN STRAUSS
Sense and Nonsense about Prayer

We are surrounded by God's benefits.
The best use of these benefits is
our unceasing expression of gratitude.

JOHN CALVIN
Institutes of the Christian Religion

In our daily practice of prayer,
we should begin each day with
an act of loving thankfulness to God.

C. F. ANDREWS
Christ and Prayer

We well know that the divine mercy
outran our best memory,
yet we should be forever blessing the Lord.

W. GRAHAM SCROGGIE
Method in Prayer

When I go to God, I want to thank Him,
first and most,
for the kindness that remembers me
even when I forget Him.

ARTHUR GOSSIP
In the Secret Place of the Most High

I really can praise You that
You refuse to let us stay children,
that You keep insisting on our growing up.

CATHERINE MARSHALL
Something More

I have learned a great deal about prayer,
praying for other people when the need arises,
spontaneously and immediately. . . .
We can share with each other without
being threatened by each other's differences
because we know that we are united by Christ,
and this union is a union of love and not fear.

MADELEINE L'ENGLE
The Rock that Is Higher

It is in the union and fellowship of believers
that the Spirit can manifest His full power.

ANDREW MURRAY
With Christ in the School of Prayer

Many a time when I've been dead tired,
I've joined a group for prayer
and so forgotten myself that at the end
I've been amazed to find myself
rested and relaxed.

HELEN SMITH SHOEMAKER
Prayer and You

God likes to see His people shut up to this,
that there is no hope but in prayer.
Herein lies the Church's power against the world.

ANDREW BONAR
The Diary and Life of Andrew Bonar

Can you imagine what could happen if
all across this country groups of church members
not only prayed for their pastors,
but became channels through whom
the Holy Spirit could flow toward pastors?

TONY CAMPOLO
Wake Up America

The devil smiles when we make plans.
He laughs when we get too busy.
But he trembles when we pray—
especially when we pray together.

CORRIE TEN BOOM
Don't Wrestle, Just Nestle